Lovable CATS & DOGS
COLORING BOOK

Ruth Soffer

DOVER PUBLICATIONS, INC.
MINEOLA, NEW YORK

What could be more lovable than a purring cat or a playful puppy? If you adore these four-legged companions, these 31 charming images will be sure to warm your heart. Especially intended for advanced colorists, these illustrations feature the animals amidst intricate outdoor landscapes. Drawings include a fashionable wirehair cat sporting a bonnet, a chihuahua in a flower pot, a trio of cats in the garden, and a Shar Pei nuzzling a bunny. After coloring, remove the perforated pages from the book and display these cherished furry friends for everyone to see.

Bibliographical Note

Lovable Cats and Dogs Coloring Book is a new work, first published by Dover Publications, Inc., in 2016.

International Standard Book Number

ISBN-13: 978-0-486-80445-3
ISBN-10: 0-486-80445-3

Manufactured in the United States by RR Donnelley
80445302   2016
www.doverpublications.com

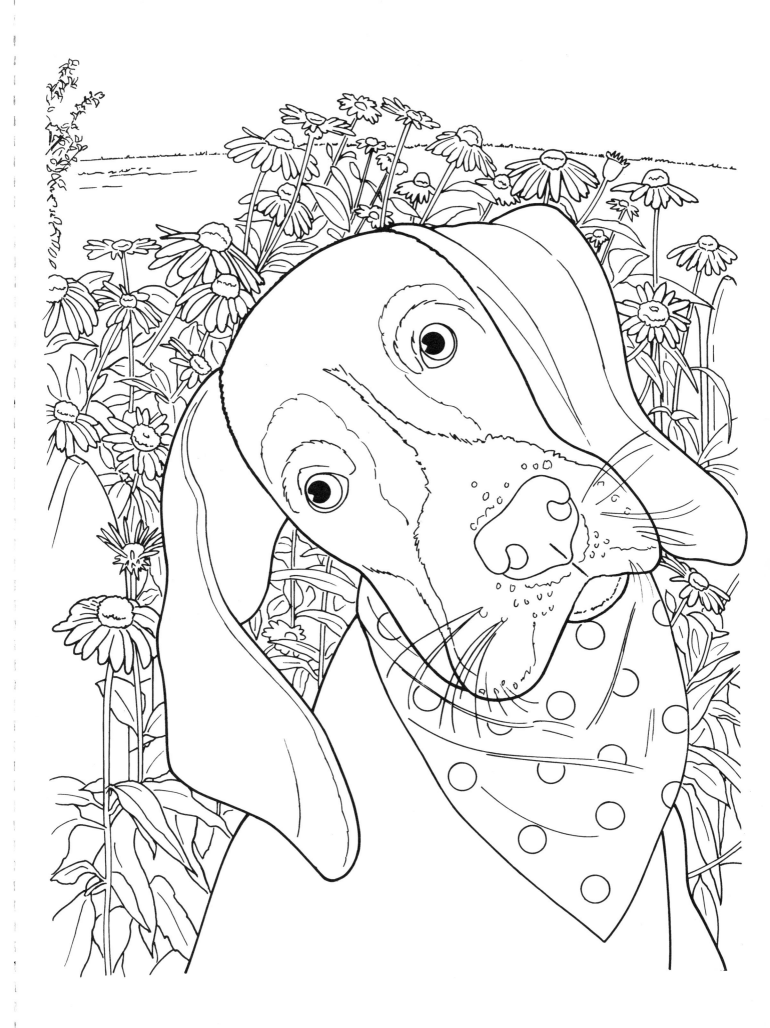

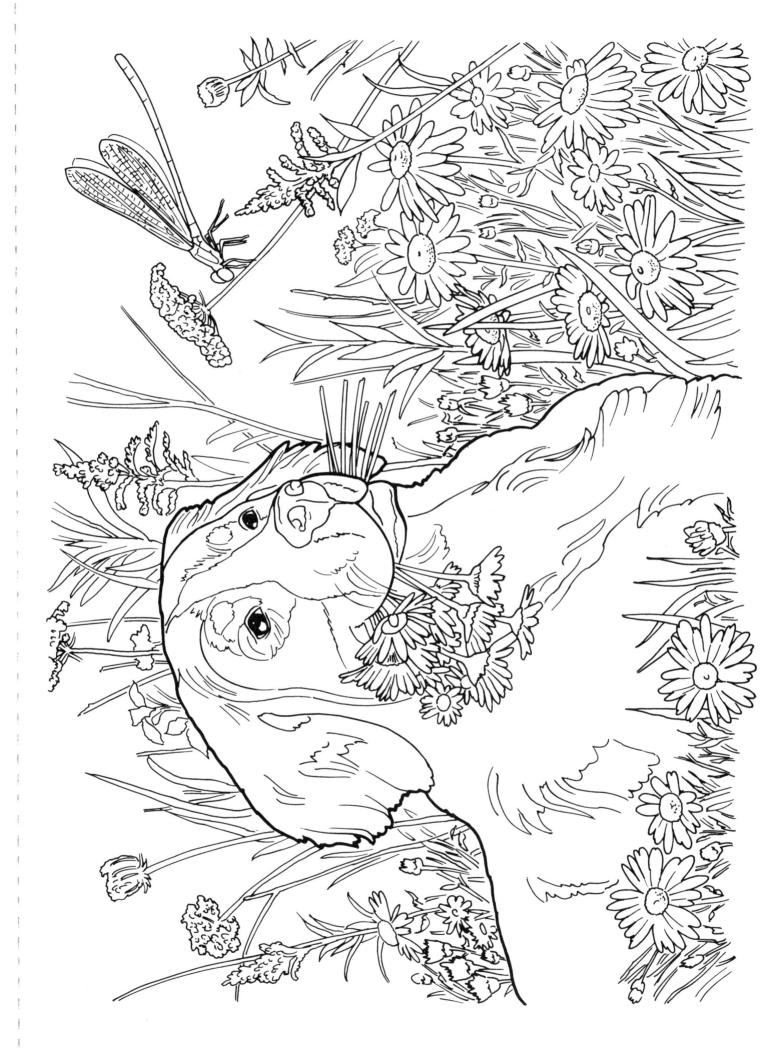